LATCH

Rebecca Goss is a poet, tutor and mentor living in Suffolk. Her first full-length collection, *The Anatomy of Structures*, was published by Flambard Press in 2010. Her second collection, *Her Birth* (Carcanet/Northern House, 2013), was shortlisted for the 2013 Forward Prize for Best Collection, won the Poetry category in the East Anglian Book Awards 2013, and in 2015 was shortlisted for the Warwick Prize for Writing and the Portico Prize for Literature. In 2014, Rebecca was selected for the Poetry Book Society's Next Generation Poets. Her second pamphlet *Carousel*, a collaboration with the photographer Chris Routledge, was published by Guillemot Press in 2018. Rebecca's third full-length collection, *Girl*, was published with Carcanet/Northern House in 2019 and shortlisted for the East Anglian Book Awards 2019. She has an MA in Creative Writing from Cardiff University and a PhD by Publication from the University of East Anglia.

Latch

Rebecca Goss

CARCANET POETRY

FOR MY PARENTS

'and I, in my brand new body,
which was not a woman's yet,
told the stars my questions'

ANNE SEXTON
from 'Young'

First published in Great Britain in 2023 by
Carcanet
Alliance House, 30 Cross Street
Manchester, M2 7AQ
www.carcanet.co.uk

A CIP catalogue record for this book is
available from the British Library.

ISBN 978 1 80017 321 7

Book design by LiteBook Prepress Services
Printed in Great Britain by SRP Ltd, Exeter, Devon

The publisher acknowledges financial
assistance from Arts Council England.

CONTENTS

LATCH

THE HOUNDS

It's as if something
calamitous is coming.

Their lament
rising across fields,

its claim on the dawn
keeping all the birds silent.

I want to know what stirs them,
the force of this pack.

What causes them to stand,
muscled frames trembling,

throats full of baleful song.
I am wakeful, rapt

and disrupted, their bays
sonorous against glass.

Should I slide the thin pane,
push my upper body

into emerging light,
let them scent out my sex,

tell them
we are all afraid.

O this night, this bidding,
claws at the latch,

pure thunder of them running,
my mouth opening

to the cool
and agitated air.

NEST

The cygnets draw a crowd
before they are born.
Mother swan's occasional
rise to nudge her ovate crop,
beak slow and practised
at the turning. Father swan
circling, rearing at dogs.

We return to see one, peeping,
puff of grey from under her
and the next week come back
to find a family gone. One,
unhatched, remaining.
Its marble lonely in the bowl.
Your hand slips out of mine

as you bolt to waiting swings,
leaving me with the egg, and all mothers
who lay their babies down, knowing
they cannot stay beside them,
must lower their own bodies into water
and continue with the swim.

STARS IN A FIELD

I have asked for this county
to soften in you

your marrow to swim

with its flint and barley
that you learn villages

and their stiles

sense the shadows
of churches

want stars in a field

bend to its soils
black and alluvial

swallow all the coasts

salt in our kisses
close a cottage door

stay with me behind it

THE PACT

Hay, recently harvested, turned to those sweet-smelling
blocks, barn-stacked, almost to the roof, forbidden.
Only the dog watched our clamber, taking us
to where the swallows come, and up there
we leapt and trod the dry bundles, our elevated play.
Then one of us was gone. Slipped unnoticed into a gap
our parents warned us of, how this strawy structure
could snatch a boy, or girl, and the plummet too great,
too narrow to save them. We needed to hear him
before we laid our chests at the edge of the hole, my arm
voted longest to stab into the deep, a reaching into myth
where I felt his plump hand and heaved, watched his flop
into the light. Circled, shaking, we tried to still our
breathing, made the necessary promise, headed back
to the house and kitchen, mother cooking, the fall a secret
held far into our adult lives. Forever haunted by it morphing.
The drop deeper, our mother unable to remember
what made her look out of the window. Maybe she felt us
coming, or maybe our approaching shadows interfered
with the light. Standing at the glass, the smell of leek
and potato soup suddenly strong yet she ignored its simmer
to watch her children, running. Middle boy screaming.
She couldn't hear it but could tell by the stretch of his mouth.
Middle girl behind him, struggling to keep up, glasses loose
on her face. Eldest leading the terrible flee, white pumps
spitting gravel. The barn looming in black behind them,
unable to see her youngest boy, her youngest boy not with them,
her youngest boy not pulled from that warm well.

COUSINS

They were meant to know each other
in this piece of countryside.

They were meant to clamber its stiles,
show us the fields as they saw them.

They were meant to know seasons,
conduct fair-headed inspections of bark,

coevals at a river's edge. They were
meant to know distance and run ahead

with the dog. They were meant to know
birdsong and bracken and bees.

They were meant to know each other,
charting these lanes like we did.

They were meant to know rain
and slowworms, the berries

that bleed in a palm. They were
meant to climb – my heart tipped –

come back down and argue
in the race to the ford.

They were meant to know rabbits
torn, opened, and a muntjac's stare

before the vanish into bramble.
They were meant to learn tracks

and to leave them, and to know
what it is to be lost. They were

meant to know each other, come to me
with a clutch of cow parsley's lace.

THE FARM

Semi-derelict, ramshackle whimsy of a place. Our father
transplanting his family at the end of a track, huddle of empty
barns, field after field, no heating. Moving in at New Year,

my sister and I in kilts and patent Mary Janes, delivered
fresh from the pantomime by Grandma who slipped our feet
into plastic loaf bags fixed at the ankles with elastic bands,

waded us through the brown flood that led to the house.
Our mother ready, belly swollen with number four, beds made,
no curtains, thickest dark outside. The frequent tipping of us

out of the kitchen into barn, meadow, stream with its
fluctuating depths. Her trust in the countryside unwavering.
Rush of snow deadening the valley. Our father attaching

sledge to tow bar, each of his children, in turn, skyrocketing
through cold. His erratic presence accepted. Our mother
loading us into the car at night, in rain, driving 300 yards

to get barn-stored coal. Cats who never came indoors. Fifty hens.
Dog roaming for bitches. The school bus dropping me at the end
of the track, older boys mooning from the rear window, my scarlet

shame at their pale arses. Walking in the back door, past our mother,
her long phone calls, her crying. Children nestled, dirty, barefoot.
Her shouting. Her transformations. Wellies kicked off to wear

the night sky on her feet: peep toe, diamanté studded heels, with bow.
The most beautiful things I had seen in my life. The swirl
of her black silk Marilyn Monroe dress, her marriage almost over.

ROOKS

Dozens, dozens, as if shaken from a blanket,
your head tilted right back, watching
this noisy announcement of bedtime, black scrawl

squawking in gusto. Freewheeling against sky's
deep orange streaks, breathy trails of cloud
and it's so easy for them to dip down, swarm,

feathers at the young tendons of your neck,
cotton at your shoulders nipped in very lengthy
beaks, that sudden rush as ground goes. Child lifted

to spend dusk in the walnut tree, not as sacrifice
but as guest, so keen are they to share the comfort
of a steady branch, demonstrate the act of roost,

the relief of reaching somewhere safe. I sip my tea
and think about waving. Gloss of dark heads eclipsing
your cheek. Sweet pitch of your chattering, twigs in your hair.

BLACKSMITH, MAKING

I met a man fluent
in the lexicon of spark
and watched him stand, forge-lit,
waiting for the brightest yellow.
Brief glares to tell
what's buried in the coke.
I witnessed steel's
blazed compliance in the vice,
neared an anvil's kept heat,
saw the dips and rust
upon its face. I heard
the hammer's bounce and strike
and bounce again.
Felt myself to be occupied
by the chime of it.
I held a latch, full of purpose
and his thinking.

DARLIN'

When I heard it said
in affection,
the roll of its 'r'
in an accent
that ages a man
by a decade,
I heard the river
of this town in his throat.
I caught the harvests,
lanes and banks of this track
as they came tumbling out.

I fell alongside,
eyes always on the dogs,
soon learned
that his 67 years
were lived here. Feats made
in a radius of four roads.
An excellent life, darlin'.

I thought of my split
from this county,
the stench of pastoral
swallowed
in a city's current.
How I stayed away so long.

who was happy to slip away walk with me into the back field
where I drank her 17-year-old wisdom could look at her
hair the opposite colour of mine her blue jeans convincing
myself my twelve years were not an issue both of us plucking
at grasses when we got almost to the oak we ventured back to
the adults neither of us missed I lost Susie in the drunken stir
of my parents' garden until night got ready to flood the party
I thought I might go in search of her or the cats so went to
the furthest barn and in the black that had rolled inside I saw
Susie being held by Richard the boy I'd ignored because his
punky clothes confused me now his left hand inside Susie's
back pocket as they sought each other's mouths air urgent
unfamiliar standing there considering myself betrayed waiting
until breakfast to utter it the sudden turn of my parents' heads
curious to know what I saw my mother sensing something
flicker staring at her daughter so full of heat and blood and
questions

WHAT WILL IT BE LIKE TO BE HERE?

Your future tallness
is evident as we pass
on a narrow landing,
bannister rail low
at your hip. Soon
you will undress,
pulling off clothes,
your arms
knocking on beams,
a ceiling too close
for your stretch.
This will be
all you have known,
and I fear it will be
too small for you.
These walls
of wool and daub
not enough
to bring us privacy.
I do not know how
I will love your father
at night. Your own secrets
a room away
you will no doubt
hate it here,
for its oldness, for everything
it lacks. And I will love it
for the years it gave me,
watching you come down
steep stairs, a spill of toys
from your lap, to be met

by the dog at the foot.
Until you grow to test my faith
in jowl posts, your limbs
straining at the structure, like Alice,
head and neck bowed by beams.
Neighbours will wonder the magic of you –
your hair pouring
from a bedroom window,
your lips angry at the old, cold glass
and I'll be downstairs,
my eye level with the bliss
of your ankle, my tiny voice
calling your name, praying
for this timber frame to bear us.

WOMAN RETURNS TO CHILDHOOD HOME, CARRIES OUT AN ACT OF THEFT

I tell you it's the stream I'd like to
see again. Body of running water,
unchanged. Its minor force continuous,

still shallow, bubbling. Leaves
in their race over small greening rocks.
Field's longest margin. Incessant edge

I adhered to. Place of no shouting.
Place of barefoot wading and other
harmless actions. I bend down

to find it surprisingly compliant.
Translucent rope, wound, gathered,
heavy as a baby by the time I reach the car,

hoping that when I say goodbye
you won't notice the dampness of my sleeves.
Fourth gear, its small waterfalls noisy

on the back seat, squirming free of the seatbelt
to purl at my neck. I try to explain to my husband
the need to smuggle in this water,

why I need it to eddy at the foot of our bed.
He says he will help me scoop the last bends
from the footwell. We watch it run about the house,

searching its new level, small stones tumbling,
until it feels like it has always quivered here.
I picture you, bewildered, pacing the dry bed.

Nothing but your shoes kicking at soil.

MY FATHER GAVE A COCKEREL TO JACK BRUCE

In return he invited us for supper. His house
buried in a lost Suffolk lane, garden rambling,

rooms warm with worn textiles, the comfort of things.
His young children playing in that familiar

wild way my siblings and I knew about. Jack cooked.
Pea soup. Its tureen brought to the table

where he poured sparkling wine into its centre,
set it frothing, mouths agog at our bowls.

My seventeen-year-old self, indifferent
to old rock stars, couldn't fathom why

there was so little talk of the French A Level
I was expected to sit in the morning.

I didn't care about cockerels either. Possessive
of fifty hens, could be a nasty fucker, flying

at my sister when she carried in the feed.
Dad and Jack, spoons forgotten,

finding their conversational riff.
My mum, charming, leaning her beautiful,

freckled arms across the table,
the whole night calling him Bruce Jack.

AFTER HARVEST IN THE EIGHTIES

                                        Farmer's dip to the straw. Flame's catch.

Slow crackle, building to tall rage. Four of us, paper dolls,
                        thrilled by stubble burning.

        Riddance of sunned-stubs
that scratched at our ankles,

        bloodied our socks
during the chase.

        We lure it. Fire's reel
                        over field.
                                        Blaze of its roll
                                                close to the house.

        Fear its leap of the fence.

That night, soil blackening.
                        House flanked by smoulder. In the news, men are striking
                Striking out. Black valleys full of anger.

                        Our mother is bent
        at bedroom floors, in slow reaping.
                                                We are her wild
                                                and tended things.

She must carry the smoky shapes of us.

WE SAW DEER

having tunnelled amber
colours of the lane and turned
the blind bend

there she was, her tiptoe
from hedge to field,
three fawn ahead of her.

I slowed, pressed the button
to slide your window down
heard our car's diesel notes

as she ushered them
across soil's cracked folds,
tawny limbs of her young, nimble

and almost at the copse
but her deliberate pause
to look back at us, the quiet muscle of her

wanting us gone,
field too wide, too baring,
her stare a fuck-you in the daylight,

my daughter's respectful
lowering of her phone.
The high windows of my brother's house

also witness to the final bolt,
talk of *did you see them?*
as we unfolded ourselves

from the car, knowing
why he chose this place,
our children fleeing into the afternoon.

SISTER, WITH MOLE

Kept for a day in scruffy
Barbour pocket,

your only ally
in ten acres.

Kept with you
in pebbled stream

and in clover. With you
to find food,

leaf-plate of worm, berry.
Mole spading

at your lap,
your fingers busy

in an early act
of raising.

Your own children
born when you

tell me this.
Mole not knowing

the heat of adult voices.
Mole safe

in that hushed
barn space.

It was dusk,
and nobody called for you.

WEIR

Boys coax as she stands at the edge
in her underwear, body taut, teenage,
the boys' skins wet from already jumping
and she's letting them look at her, knowing
the power she has, and we have only just
moved to this town, this river new, its cold
unknown and you are in your buggy, shoes
kicking their pink in front of me and I think
how soon it will be before the splash, boys
looking at you in the water, breath held,
your legs weaving black reeds, unfetched.

CLOSE WORK

You take off the old,
and what crumbles

uncovers birds, coins,
hats rested for centuries.

Often clay pipes,
where men before you

paused in equal summer heat
because it taxes the limbs

this work to strip poor lime,
dress my house

from the feet up with flossy bulge
of sheepswool.

Your forefinger's rough tip
measures the gap

between laths; the pluck
of ring shank nail

from a leather pouch
at your hip.

It is labour you repeat:
place, gauge, pin, knock

whilst crouched
on a bucket upturned

and once you have finished
the restoration of shape

a bandaging in oak,
it will be your wrist

bearing the weight
of wet lime, hawk heavy

with hair, chalk, water.
How benign plaster looks

the inviting
sludge of its cream

but too long on your palms
it has burned.

The minor cargo of tools:
trowels, small and worn-in,

biddable to the veer
as the building pulls you

around its frame. A scratch coat's
score of lines for key,

the seeming ease
with which you sweep.

My walks in the wheatfield
waiting for a wall to dry,

fingers floating over awn,
dropping down

to the street of coloured houses
and from gate to garden

I smooth my hand
against its cool.

STATE OF BEING YOUNG

With two pairs of jeans, rammed
in a paper bag, splitting, and a fury
so palpable birds felt it.
Her leaving not yet an absence,
not yet felt in the din.
She had made her half-escape,
a sharp bend beckoning.
For the girl at the end of the track
the wait felt everlasting
before her mother came,
car stuffed with siblings,
the wobble of their heads
as tyres sunk into every pothole
and rose again. Passenger door
pushed open in surrender,
the gesture saying
don't leave us now, not yet.
You are the eldest, and alarmed
at many things, but come home
to be a girl a little longer.
Bring the hate and disappointment
with you, tuck it here beside the seat
and we'll drive home for hot chocolate,
the kitchen table still strewn
with a week's dishes, the day's mud
on quarry tiles, dog splayed at the range.
We may forgive each other.

WHEN IT FEELS HOT, THAT RAGE AGAINST ME

will I tell you of the pitch-black mile
        walked with cidery mouths, our hair
   flushed in occasional headlight, throats singing

Sweet Child O' Mine, a distance increasing
        from men we left at the pub, too old, too
   frightening when they did react to the early

curve of our bodies. My mother elsewhere
        in the starlit hinterland, just the lane knowing
   how to hold us, its chorus of night creatures.

The collapse into a bedroom, joint
        a shared firefly at our lips, clothes strewn,
   soon sleeping like children. I will understand

your need to be away from me and with girls,
        girls I want to wake now, pull from
   the men they chose, pull from their tumble-dried sheets,

become a multitude storming under stars, sky crackling
        at the sight of us, all the promises re-rising
   in our throats, needing each other like fire.

WOMAN RETURNS TO CHILDHOOD HOME, FINDS HERSELF AMONGST OTHERS

You're narrating thirteen years here,
cat stepping casually over our cake
when I notice my mother behind you,

scarf silky in her red hair as she bends
to turn down the boxy television's volume,
my bearded father leaning against the room's

brick arch, orange balloons bumping his feet
and while you're talking walls turn from cream
to terracotta, my mother bringing plate after plate

from the chaos of the kitchen for her friends
gathering behind your head in their hats
and fabulous trousers, the fine fog

of their cigarettes over your shoulder,
my brothers' wooden trikes heading for
people's ankles and when I look outside

I see my uncle crying and this is before
you've taken me to see my parents' bedroom,
looking just the same, my mother on the bed,

patting the space beside her, talking about
a car accident, the white lie she wrapped
around her brother because a gun is

unexplainable and along the landing small
brothers in the bathroom, splashing, your mouth
still moving and I'm really struggling to hear you.

DEATHWATCH BEETLES

Such a distinctive tick
to their borings,
their collective, tiny strengths
causing you to poke
at what's exposed,
bring me timber crumbs.
Your day is one of heft.
My arms just able to bear
the density of our sleeping child;
her puppet limbs dangle
from my hold whereas you
can heave green oak,
brook its weight
in golden blocks, rid them
of the damp they crave
with each new, pegged splice.

Superstition says
their presence predicts
a death, but death
is something we are versed in.
Ask us, and we will
wax lyrical into the night,
all nights, about pale rooms
that have kept us,
how the breath of a child
or father or wife or mother
or sister can narrow
until those rooms release
a stillness, pure, almost needed.

Lie with me, after the moil

and I will tell you
their knocking is a call to love.
It is not death but longing,
in miniature, many of them
spent by morning, speckled
upon carpet and our books.
Our child collects curled
husks, prehistoric in the pink
of her palm. You kneel
before her fingers, say
it's when she's dreaming that
they fall to her from beams.

THE RETIRED AGRONOMIST DRIVES A TRACTOR IN THE SUMMER BECAUSE HE LIKES THE OILY SMELL OF THE MACHINE

And how the soil turns
to give up its creaturely
yield. Gulls, massing.
Their swoops to raid each
cultivated ridge. And how
unchanged it is for bird
to follow plough. Purest wings
dipping down to earth.
And how his wife crosses
stubble to bring pasta with
green beans from the garden,
three spaniels at her heels.
And how this meal is eaten
in the tractor's cab after
oilseed rape is sown, fruiting.
And how we will pass
this laboured square, remark
the yellow dazzle.

CREOSOTE

Two decades before its ban, one tabby cat
misjudged a leap, fell into an open bucket,
no doubt struggled in the tarry splash,
caused an eventual tip and dragged its
saturated body from barn to gravel,
not quite reaching the gate. Up early
to feed him, I found him, tacky, wheezing,
and ran to my parents, asleep, knelt at my
father's side to shake his bare shoulder
so that he woke to find me sobbing, saying
something's happened, something's happened
and he dressed quickly for me to pull him
into Sunday, into sunlight, and I don't even know
if he wore gloves to lift him, still breathing,
lungs of midnight, into the car, my mother
watching, calling me back into the house.

PHEASANT IN REAR-VIEW MIRROR

Only I see it,
running the width
of the glass, parting grasses
in eager scurry,
its plumage a spectacle
and your shiny fringe
bobbing in the foreground.

We are about to make our way
inside a wood,
parked at its entrance
yet I let the engine
tick a little longer, this encounter
holding a small significance,
your limbs yet to realise

we are stationary,
that you can soon
escape your seat and enter
through the kissing gate;
the bird you never saw gone,
its iridescence
a failing flare in the meadow.

The click of a car seat unbuckling.
You have made your decision
to leave this space,
because inside the car with your mother
you won't see
Brimstone butterflies,
the seasonal ponds,

the coppiced limes'
determined stretch towards light.
It's hard to understand
that you ever step on pavements,
as you skip beyond
the gate's kind admission
into a realm that knows

my wish to stay within its hold,
sees your hair
lit by what can filter
from above,
your body appearing
and vanishing in succession;
a bird sighted,
thrilled at, then flown.

YOUR THUMB AT THE LATCH

its soft press
releasing
a lever bar

nursing its own
distinctive
click, so I know

which door's frame
holds you briefly
as you duck

your head,
this house needing
a lean

into each room
then the murmur
of voices

drifting up
through boards
father   child

talking
in a motherless
space

my body upstairs
sheltered
in warm,

quiet water
knees raised
to study

last week's
bruise, touching
the blue hurt

in a state
of absence,
heart set

to know you
pushing
between rooms.

LANE

Width of one car,
our car,
swallowing grass

that thrives in a strip
at its centre
and from verges

a lean of wild heads
leading us,
rare callers,

around each blind
bend, this twisting aisle
with its utter lack

of sign, or streetlight
or markings
yet is valid track,

ditch-edged, meandering,
tunnels of high
branches bending,

then out into
fields, kite diving
bright golden

pages, hare
skittish, our eye
back to route,

meadow-spill
winding,
could be lost

but these are
verdant ghosts
guiding,

look up, daughter,
a mistake
to love this later.

BRICKS

Our house, built before
the invention of a corridor,
means my daughter leaps
from room to room,
each crooked portal taking her
to another ancient part.
I am scrubbing the brick floor
while she is at school. The window
is open, the day is hot, sweat
coats my back but I love to see
the change from black to yellow
as the bricks reveal their hue.
I'm at the part that dips,
proof of an historic door,
repeated tread.
Some bricks are cracked,
or raised at their rectangle edges
and I think of my child,
running barefoot
from one end of the house
to the other, not only able to read
this treacherous surface
with her cool soles –
(her movements sure and tidal)
but also forming her own
groove. That hundreds
of years from now, a woman
will kneel to wash these bricks,
lift my family's patina
from the clay and discover where
my daughter's weight made history.
She will feel it, smooth as bowl.

PICTURES OF YOU

I don't know if he
whispered in your ear,
the American photographer
at the dinner party where
my father was not looking
in your direction,
leaving the face of his wife
to be noticed by others

which made you
stand up from your plate, food
soft in people's mouths
to follow a camera outside,
your suede boots
laced to the knee, geometric
shapes on your skirt
sucked in one direction
by the teasing breeze

that brought you here,
my father tearing the back roads
towards an evening that saw
the red hair he loves
blown across your forehead,
your body needing no instruction,
knowing how to stir a lens,
snow white cheek tilted
into your hand. I hold
your stare and the frets
of your marital beginning.

BALES

If we run to
their curve, lie
in thin shadow,
hay's itch, good
smell, field
shimmer, will
you see them
as I do? Dotted,
large, illusory,
overly gold.

BLESSINGS

There is time spent
talking about the key,
bigger than my palm,
heavy as loaf,

before the door is pushed,
its sculpted wood
in slow swing
and this is my favourite part

never knowing
what beauty or plainness
will greet me, what I will
step inside and wake.

The Reverend enters
and I follow into ornate
smallness, the light
we have disturbed

reflecting its kiss
on polished wood, tiles, brass.
We choose a pew and let it
keep us, as it keeps your

tiny congregation
who walk past meadow, mere,
to evensong, sit beneath
stone sills, candles shivering

through hymns and I'm believing
I will come, bring my family,
show them how easy it is
to feel cherished here.

A farm on the outskirts stores a pool where the water looks greenish and Sylvia, half-submerged takes my daughter by the scruff of her costume, arm floats cast off, slices her through water. The format irregular, yet generations of a town have learnt this way. Soon, my daughter's dive with eager grace, the splashless vanish of her pencil-jump. The time we drove Sylvia home. Single-track road and her chatter. Fields listening. She came to Suffolk at night. Stepped onto the bus with her mother. From Peckham to this one town, decades pending in its sky. Found Mrs Norman, housing mothers in the aftershock of war. Mrs Norman's half-dozen children of her own stood in nightgowns. Whitest cotton falling from chin to toe and Sylvia thought that she had died, thought she'd got to Heaven, six angels there to greet her. We stop at the bungalow. I carry her things to the door. Drive home, bloom of her damp outline on the seat.

She can see the back of his head. His Morris Traveller still facing up the lane, elbow out the window as he views his crops. Tweed-covered shoulders familiar as morning. She lowers her bike to the ground, calls out his name and so my grandma finds her father dead in the driver's seat, face struck by the sun. She waits before climbing beside him, listens to the same birds who sung to him, watches the harvest in lazy, yellow light. She lifts his face, lets her fingers feel him for a second then starts the engine and in reverse gear steers him home. The car bumps down the track, his head rolling onto her shoulder, tweed cap scratching her chin but she lets him stay there, against her, until they reach the farmhouse, everyone inside for his birthday, expecting his amble back for wine and the half-eaten cake.

REARING

We are driving to a juvenile plantation,
a mere twenty-five years up from the ground

but first must negotiate the cows, their nearing
amber bulk, vast heads slow with sunshine.

You laugh at my unease, steer the buggy round
until eventually the ground begins to dip,

and a heron guides us in. With its shadow flung
I envy that aerial view, how it gets to see

these scattered blooms of woodland
as it swoops the farm's square mile.

We find a trunk, moss-ridden, prone, and sit.
For a short time, the labour in you, idle.

These are lush and secret places you have made,
fishing the bowls of dark water, lakes you dug

edged with skinny tilt of sycamore, sweet chestnuts
climbing for sky. What I know about nurture

is proved in the gait of a nine-year-old child,
long-limbed and thriving, her hair's fast slip

around my fingers as if I knelt to tear
the surface and pulled her from this deep.

WOMAN RETURNS TO CHILDHOOD HOME, REMEMBERS

that it was almost light
when my father walked out
to find her. From my window

I watched the faint beam
of his torch, steady,
until he started running,

field swallowing him whole.
When he brought my mother
home she was already

undressing. Soon she was naked
from the waist down. Her tight,
adult limbs pale and frightening

as she negotiated the landing
towards me. Her mouth had a new,
difficult smell. She carried

a glass bottle, quarter full
and sloshing. I wanted her
far away, back out in the field

where the dark could wrap
round her, ease her into sleep
until I woke her in the morning.

I'd have food in my bag,
we could eat breakfast
in the high grass and she

could plait my hair beneath
the oak tree, acorns forming
above us in their cups.

UNDER A NEW SKY

everything is
smaller. grief diminishes
to a more manageable form.
the vast changes
in scenery. how required
they were. to wake in a
different house. shop
in a different town. speak
with different people.
my girl up sticked.
coming to where her
mother grew. must create
her own associations
with this county. make tremors
of its light

TO LOVE A GAMBREL ROOF

Like a bonnet,
cupping barn sides
with its two tiled slopes

granting a farmer more
storage and me my
Playmobil recollections.

Beneath it
loft and stalls,
a watering trough,

maybe a horse
with satisfyingly
moveable joints.

Seen from the road,
the consolation
of its shape in the field,

the red of the walls
that hold it.

ARGER FEN

You packed with some certainty:
toy fox, binoculars,

small notebook,
the biro-of-many-colours.

I hold your hand on the path,
recall when here was wilder.

No posts bearing green arrows,
no designated trail.

I'd come with my sister
and brothers, for the heavy

heads of bluebells, oblivious
to Goat's-beard, Colt's Foot,

Hoary Ragwort, all around us
the stuff of spells. Our parents

let us go to scamper deeper,
leap from stumps lush with moss.

Everything aloof about me
fell into the soil once charged

with younger siblings
and freedoms of a wood.

Now here you are, with your pen,
keen to label each bird's call.

I give you a damp valley floor,
this feather for your pocket.

VIOLET

We bring your daughter to you, Violet,
though she is dust and ashes –
and settle our shoes on uneven ground,
listen to birdsong before Reverend Hallett
reads from a soft, black book.

She was sixteen the day you died,
that page in her diary left blank
but her will, spread upon my father's desk,
revealed a plea. So my parents drove
the grassy cambers to St Lawrence,

wandered its wilder parts: nettles
tall as children, tombstones crumbled
into moss, and found it, Ellen Violet Brewer,
tilted, where the yew tree spills its shade.
A letter was composed, a day arranged.

Sixty-five years since your committal
to this bucolic patch, we come as a congregation
of three. My whole childhood, drifting
these lanes but never treading into this one.
Until Reverend Hallett greets us

at its isolated curve, leads us to a settlement
of weeds, a plot of dug-up dirt, commends
my grandmother to the ground, so you, Violet,
can draw your daughter down.

MAKERS OF LADDERS

Before the climb
and the hauling of the straw,

a thatcher must relinquish us
his foot. Then, we can note

the scale between instep
and his knee –

the fleshy part that yields
beneath the cap.

That way,
the spacing of the rungs

will bear his kneeling,
as he pushes spar

and crook in place.
Made from ash (cut

between two moons
ensuring sap has fallen

from the trunk)
this makes a stronger stilt –

curved inside, so he can brace himself
on round.

Up there, his steps are tailored, steady
as he reaches over eaves,

finds marsh beneath the recoats
and rush and flax and broom.

Dodo took a pip and planted you. Dodo who lived here before me. Dodo who had weekly bonfires and secret drawers and possibly put meat in the compost. Dodo watched you grow from the conservatory. Two decades of watching. Her last plum eaten at 104, house falling quiet. Then I came, shouldered boxes into cupboards, vestiges I can't look at but won't destroy. Afterwards sat under your crooked branches and cried, worms plumping on grief. Then you turned bountiful. Purple jewels, sweet and profitable. Small child at the gate selling ten at a time. I don't know how I have come to outlive things. Learning today that a plum tree spans twenty years of life, I worry at your spent branches. Please be the rare exception. See the child with her book beneath you, see her benefit from your shade.

WE WALK THIS AVENUE OF ENGLISH OAK

to count twenty-six.
one tilting.
only a tractor
Planted to mark
of tenure, this route
your brother's
Sheep are languid
against a given
your father sited
he would never
see your children
between each gate,
sleep out here

One dead,
After the storm's roar
could heave it back.
your family's centenary
connects two houses,
and your own.
as you lean
limb, tell me
saplings knowing
wander under, or
born to course
let them
with owls.

THERE WAS A SWING

and my father claimed it.
His teenage frame
leant into the rope,
links of chance around him:

a friend called Pip,
Pip's garden, the liberty of summer.
She came through gates,
poised herself on the lawn

and from his sway, my father
saw my mother. How long he waited
before he rose, I don't know,
but as the party began its swell

the blonde boy wandered
closer to the red-headed girl.
Her beauty was outright
and everywhere – in her hair,

her freckled arms, in her skin
still holding the day's heat.
Eloquent, head-cocked,
he made her laugh until she slowed

his burgeoning swagger
with the murmur of her voice.
They danced most of the night
this girl, this boy,

both still at school,
a marriage unimagined,
home unmade,
their children stars away.

I HEAR THIS RINGING FROM MY HOME

It leaves some breathless, the heave.
Both underarm and clavicle conscious of the tug.
With twenty-eight hundredweight of chime
you have to *feel* the bell, and they say
it takes ten thousand pulls before
you can claim to do it right. It begins with
spiralled stone: ninety-three wedged, uneven steps
make for cautionary climb but once inside the tower
they bustle under rafters, quite devoted
and intent. Fingers curled around a sally,
the mandatory hush before a sudden
syncopated freeing from the bronze, a ringing
under clouds, my absolute ascending into sound.

FIELD FIRE

Having begun
        as a flint snicked

sharp blue edge
        unseen in sunned barley

struck by machinery
        to become tinder

spark after spark
        blonde dust

of the combine
        morphing to black plume

standing crops flame
        a flash across road

car's brush
        with the end of things

talk of this in kitchens
        the day cast on warm floors.

WE ARE BURIED UNDER LIME

Before the tender episodes
of our deaths, and the emptying
as if we were hardly here

I wrap our story, watch it drown
beneath horsehair and chalk.
Your letter, tucked with a newspaper

and postcard of this market town.
The craftsmen who paused their tools
to add their trade and autograph.

It will take half a century of weather
to expose us, a gift from the fault.
When the wall splits, they'll find

your infant-school hand describing
a household: what a mother does,
what a father does, your drawing of the dog.

They'll see news was cast in papery sheets,
a High Street car-filled and industrious.
I hope they carry the packet to the garden,

that there is a garden and from there look up
at the house, see a poet inside, turning her face
to a carpenter, taking the hand of their child.

IN SONG FLIGHT

Sky shepherd,
watching me in barley,

you are ringing,
risen,

hidden in the blue.
I look up

to see cloud,
wavering.

Am I leading,
or are you?

This walk,
with tremolo

at my crown,
sermon

of gold prospect.
Render me

woken,
bring me home.

GATE

Here she comes,
hair a stream,
path home, dog's
ears pricked
to the latch,
and I'm in the
garden, pear tree
spilling, day of poems
behind me, hiding

my stored dark,
thinking
I must look old
and not extraordinary,
her skin the truest surface
wanting to kiss her
as she drops
her bag, turns,
every atom of her
near me, and I
make my slight
gesture, feel
the quickening.

REPRISE

breath of dawn
all over me

and they've come,
river-wet

plunging the banks
to reach me

mouths hunting
both palms

pack's jostle,
rough tongues.

I'm smoothing
hound backs

height of small horses,
no apples

in my pocket.
How tender I am

circled by dogs.
From the window

mama mama
they close in

at this bidding,
want me

climbing
the low wall,

a wresting
to full meadow

river waiting
river waiting
river waiting

her name at my lip.

ACKNOWLEDGEMENTS

Thanks are due to the editors of the following publications in which some of these poems, or versions of them, first appeared: *Agenda, Ambit, Bad Lilies, Bath Magg, Bell House blog, London Magazine, Magma, Poetry Birmingham Literary Journal, Poetry Ireland Review, Poetry London, The Rialto*

'When It Feels Hot, That Rage Against Me' won First Prize in the 2022 Sylvia Plath Prize and was first published in *After Sylvia*, ed. Sarah Corbett and Ian Humphreys, Nine Arches Press, 2022

'Rooks' was commended in the Annual Ambit Competition 2022

'Lane' was shortlisted for The Ginkgo Prize/Areas of Outstanding Natural Beauty 'Best Poem of Landscape' 2021

'Arger Fen' first published in *Empty House: poetry and prose on the climate crisis*, ed. Alice Kinsella and Nessa O'Mahony, Doire Press, 2021

A version of 'Deathwatch Beetles' first published in *Arrival in Elsewhere*, ed. Carl Griffin, Against the Grain, 2021

'What Will It Be Like To Be Here' first published online at *WRITE Where We Are NOW*, curated by Carol Ann Duffy, Manchester Metropolitan University, 2020

A version of 'Woman Returns to Childhood Home, Remembers' first published in *The Anatomy of Structures*, Rebecca Goss, Flambard Press, 2010

Latch is for my family but also Suffolk friends, old and new. With special thanks to Anna Hills, Sylvia Barton, Dean Southernwood at DGS Plastering Ltd, blacksmith John Ball, farmer Rob Partridge at R. Partridge & Son Ltd, agronomist Robert Goodchild, Sue Goodchild, the bell ringers at St Mary's Church, Hadleigh and Reverend Liz Law, All Saints Church, Semer.

I am grateful to The Society of Authors for a Roger Deakin Award in 2016 and their financial assistance with this collection.

Huge thanks to John McAuliffe, Heidi Williamson and Helen Tookey for their insight and time. Jim, thank you for making us a home.

Finally, if I could gift a piece of Suffolk sky to anyone it would be Caroline Bird for helping me to unlock this book.